Home

Selected Poems – Volume IV

Mary Cochrane

This edition published 2018

Copyright © Mary Cochrane 2018

The moral right of the author has been asserted.

All rights reserved. No part of this publication may be reproduced, stored in a retrieval system, or transmitted in any form or by any means, without the prior permission of the copyright owner, nor be otherwise circulated in any form of binding or cover other than that in which it is published and without a similar condition including this condition being imposed on the subsequent purchaser.

ISBN: 978-1727859089

Dedicated to Joy Mawby

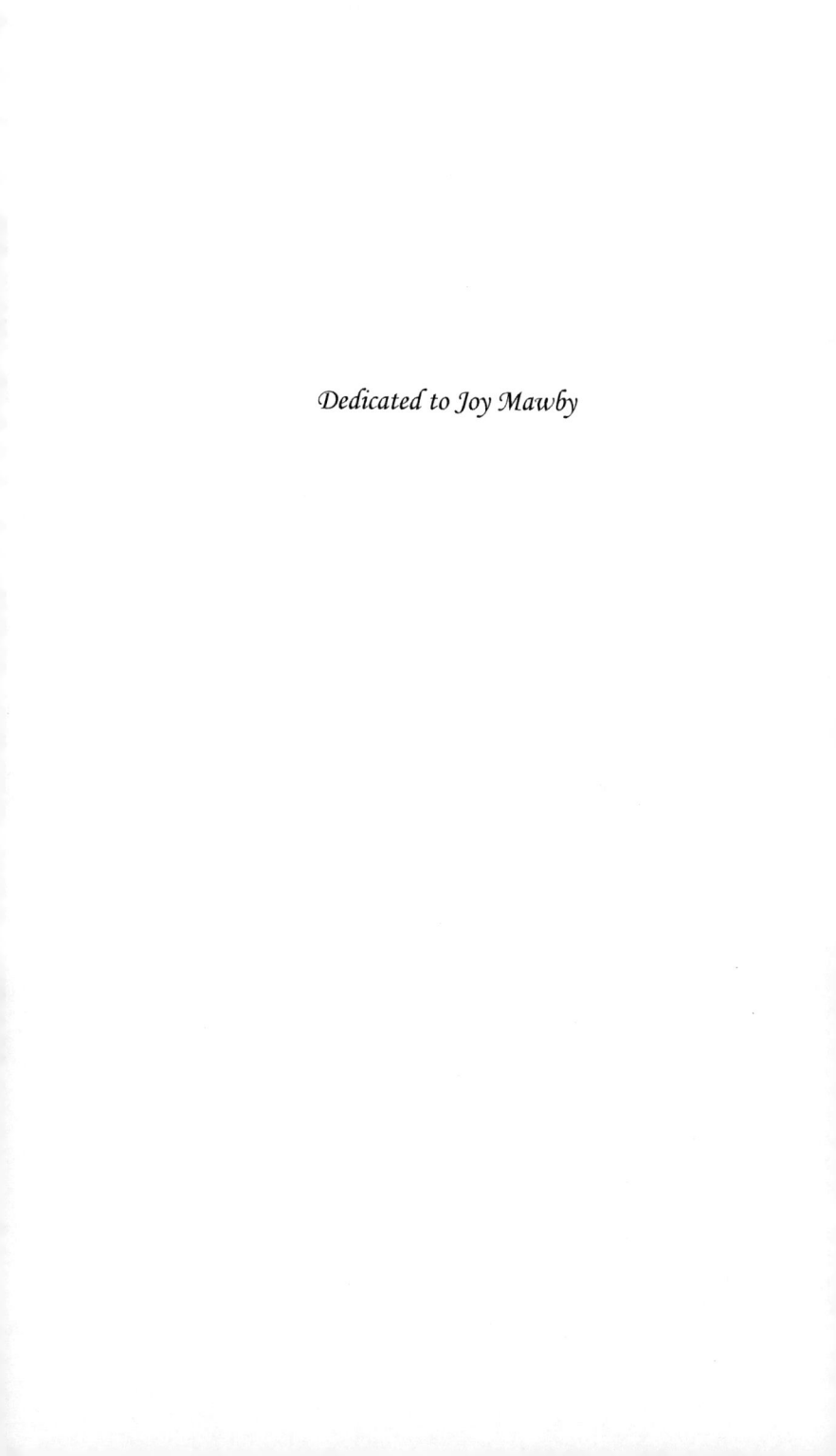

CONTENTS

Waiting	7
Not A Mere Mortal	8
The Future Waits	9
Waiting At The Wings	10
Thoughts of You	11
The Lost Vestiges of Nature	12
Haunted	13
Devoid of Living	14
Pushing Boundaries	15
Alternate Reality	16
Another Star	17
Cataclysmic Dream	18
A Better Resting Place	19
My Only Love	20
Eternal Silence	21
The Realm of the Long Lost Dead	22
Precipitous Step Into The Unknown	23
The Waiting Game	24
Chasm of Death	25
Another Hopeless Day	26
Between Worlds	27
Ghostly Presence In The Hall	28
Spark of Light	29
Life Confined	30
Lost Heritage	31
An Unfamiliar Beat	32
Bereft	33
Resignation	34
The Glittering Sword	35
Loyalty	36
Brink of An Unknown Dawn	37
Radiance	38
Fragile Landscape	39
Attainment of Truth	40
Imaginings	41

Revival	42
Pearls	43
Unfettered	44
Secrets	45
Philosophical Feast	46
Abandon	47
Up From The Skies	48
Bright Rays of Truth	49
False Hope	50
The Glittering Orb	51
Afflicted	52
Who I Am	53
Unearthly Dancer	54
Onslaught	55
Eternal Space	56
Stilled	57
Misguided	58
Nobody's Hero	59
Heady Scent of Freedom	60
Purple	61
The Great Melting Point	62
Stirrings of Life	63
Unconditionally	64
I Think of You	65
Final Moondance	67
Tantalising Glimpse	68
View of My Deeper Aspect	69
Melancholic Sense of Forever	70
Pathological Bourgeoisie	71
Dimensional Shift	72
Earthy Aroma of Youth	73
Take Me Home	74
Already Dead	75
Lost Faith In Humanity	76
What Can I Do?	77
Gateway To Liberty	78
Breathless	79

Dark Angel	80
The Life	81
Today's Bulletin	82
Anglesey Eyes	83
The Portal of Sleep	84
Passing Through	85
Debris	86
Uncharted Territory	87
The Magic of Ynys Môn	88
Inconsequential Living	89

Waiting

The sun is setting one last time -
Orange and gold surrendering
To the smooth call of darkness.

It's closing time and the chilled wine
Has inebriated the madness
Of the brave ones who have
Managed to stay for another day.

There are no loving arms in which to fall,
No soothing words to enthrall the heart;
Just the hollowness of empty rooms
And the melancholic sense of waiting.

[02.01.16]

Not A Mere Mortal

You look at my delicate features
And presume that I am feeble -
A mere mortal;
But I am not.
I will drag you with me through Heaven and
Hell,
And I will love you as you've never been loved
before.

[02.01.16]

The Future Waits

It's in the rays of the bright sun
And the faces of everyone
Who steps into your worldly view
And instigates a change in you.

It summons joy and sorrow's tears
Throughout the course of many years;
Immoveable and only seen
In the heraldic world of dreams.

With this in mind it may be wise
To set down this philosophy:
The future waits and does not bend
As you journey to its fateful end.

[09.01.16]

Waiting At The Wings

Didn't they tell you
That the sky fell down
In nineteen-ninety-five?
The world was only functioning
When he was still alive.

Didn't you see the black hole
In the space that once held
My poor shattered heart?
Didn't you know I loved him
From the very start?

Now it's just a matter
Of acting out
The final tiresome scenes;
Exiting in bliss to find him
Waiting at the wings.

[19.01.16]

Thoughts of You

I would place a little stardust
At the entrance to your residence;
Feed your hunger, sate your thirst
And bow down to your eminence.

I would fill your room with scented flowers
And help you while away the hours;
Reciting poetry and prose
As you lay in elegant repose.

I would forget the world outside:
The setting sun and stagnant tide;
The weight of time that can subdue
The heart of everyone but you.

And what of heroes and superstars?
What relevance Venus and Mars?
All life's beauty is within my view
And I'm consumed with thoughts of you.

[19.01.16]

The Lost Vestiges of Nature

There is a low and distant call
That carries on the stagnant air;
Auguring the perilous fall
Of empires with a morbid flair
For savagery and decadence
In a twisted, nihilistic quest.

There is a faint glimmer of light
That gently caresses the earth;
Awaiting the passing of night
And the frail, soporific breath
Of the multitudes who pray for
The lost vestiges of nature.

[06.02.16]

Haunted

I struggle to solidify
When your essence is passing by,
Pulling aloft my soul to dance
In a visionary trance.

Then there is the other side
Of that mercurial tide:
The body's painful colic and
The medic's unseemly rhetoric;

The sensory overload
And perpetual discord;
Contemplating one's own doom
In a solitary room.

It is a precarious line
That divides your world and mine.
I'm haunted by the sullen tone
Of a catastrophic storm.

[23.02.16]

Devoid of Living

Blood and more blood, dripping from my body;
Bright and red – a symbol of death:
My punishment for leaving London
And roaming the streets of Taunton.

I met a glamorous woman there,
In a sprawling house where I lay
On a four-poster bed, with my head
Free of turmoil and monotony.

I awoke in the night with a spectre
Bearing down upon my broken form;
Cutting through the darkness like a knife
To drag me into the afterlife:

That seemed preferable to the prospect
Of another long and lonely day;
The veil of hope slipping to reveal
The true horror of reality.

Now, the waiting begins again -
For a glimpse of moonlight or the soft voice
Laden with kindly sympathy;
Life quietly devoid of choice,

Devoid of living – impaled by blood and pain,
And in such circumstances
The spirit rises up and implores
Those charming ghosts to take me to their realm.

[29.02.16]

Pushing Boundaries

I will wait for you in a place
Without remorse, shame or conceit;
Removed from Earth, this vibrant land
Wherein we are destined to meet.

I will not utter words of love,
For love will emanate from me.
A million golden stars will light
The pathway to our sanctuary.

And never shall the weight of Earth
Impose on us morbidity:
Souls are chainless and all-consumed
With unremitting liberty.

Until that day, we must uphold
The most majestic of all dreams;
Pushing boundaries to reveal
That life is never what it seems.

[03.03.16]

Alternate Reality

All night I waited on the cove,
For you, my one true love.
The furore of the raging sea
Compounds the emptiness in me.

I barely have a breath to take
Until the sun intrudes and wakes
Me from a death-like sleep, that fades
In the weight of the world's charade.

And still I'm waiting, with the sound
Of explosions that hit the ground;
Now it's Brussels in disarray -
Another horror, another day.

Too many pathways, I cannot turn
To a previously trodden one;
I'm delving into the fantasy
Of an alternate reality.

[23.03.16]

Another Star

"We have met before. On another star,"
Joyce proclaimed in Ulysses;
Extending wisdom from the far-flung
Echelons of history.

There could be vaster places to meet
When human hope and life expire;
No mortal deeds nor death to cheat,
Nor need to sate the heart's desire.

[23.03.16]

Cataclysmic Dream

How tempting if the water
Was just within my reach;
To walk by silver moonlight
On that isolated beach.

How calmly I would go forth
And slip beneath the waves,
Immerse myself within
The subterranean maze.

The world would ebb and fade
When we met behind the scenes;
Wandering harmoniously
In a cataclysmic dream.

[12.07.16]

A Better Resting Place

Can no-one see that I'm dying?
Slowly slipping into that darkness
That mercilessly flirts with the soul.
It seems that only I can hear
The wailing of the siren's call.

But I promise to remain steadfast
In the course of these turbulent times,
If you will graciously sit with me
At the water's edge for one sweet night,
Resisting the pull of divinity:

Resisting the forces that have succeeded
In haste to carry you away.
If we should provoke the deities' distaste
And perish beneath the lightning sky,
I will bide with you in a better resting place.

[16.07.16]

My Only Love

The hours are gathering momentum;
Propelling me toward a darker fate -
One more push with renewed vigour,
Only to find that it's too late.

There is nothing left to save me;
No royal blood, fortune or fame.
The greatest frailty is stagnation
In the modern misanthropic game.

Just hold me for the longest time
And I will never seek redress.
Come back to me, my only love -
Convince me that we've conquered death.

[20.07.16]

Eternal Silence

In the cool darkness I succumb
To the delicate whisper of your soul;
Ferociously pursuing you
And denouncing this mortal role.

Since you left I have only known
A world of solitude and shadow;
Courting nihilistic phantoms
As I gradually unravel.

And through the mist I continue
To witness the thunder and violence;
Awaiting your sweet, final kiss
And the sanctum of eternal silence.

[24.07.16]

The Realm of the Long-Lost Dead

I did love you all the while,
My schizophrenic mother
With your strange, unworldly smile.

You had no diagnosis
To adequately explain
The nature of your psychosis.

I watched those terrible scenes,
Where you held my brother's mouth
To eradicate his screams;

I watched him struggle for breath
And I wept for the loss
Of our childhood innocence.

More than forty years have passed
And the wreckage of our lives
Has worn me down at last;

Sorry, but I have to say
I loved him more than other
Members of our family:

That is why I rest my head
And earnestly pray to join
The realm of the long-lost dead.

[31.07.16]

Precipitous Step Into The Unknown

Night-time seems to magnify
The enormity of it all,
And the wild vagabonds
Are vying for release
From their gloomy confines.

They respond to suppression
With fits of suffocation
And the fear of drowning
In the irrepressible
Ocean of banality:

Until the totality
Of existence is focused on
The futile quest for meaning -
Which is, at best,
Fragmented and ephemeral.

And so, back to the beginning
And the vital decision:
Hollow superficiality
Or the daring, solitary,
Precipitous step into the unknown.

[02.08.16]

The Waiting Game

If I permit you to enter
The blackest of all chambers,
Will you run and never return?
The rest have already dispersed
And the waiting game has begun.

I wander these rooms day by day,
Floundering until I sense
His ghostly presence at my side;
No comfort there or anywhere
If here I persist to abide.

Each moment is akin to battle
In the wreckage of a vessel
That was doomed to expire long ago;
And survival incomparable
To the sweetness of death's afterglow.

[04.08.16]

Chasm of Death

Blood and horrors,
Morphine and pain;
Sweet subjects you make
For this midnight refrain.

Loneliness, madness -
Submerged in the cold;
Withered and broken
Before I am old.

One sliver of hope
Before the next breath;
Fall swiftly into
The chasm of death.

[04.08.16]

Another Hopeless Day

Raise your scalpels, fellow surgeons,
And sever her body
As neatly as you can:
Perform this operation
As though you were an artisan.

No need to worry
If she cannot function
With the disability;
We will have performed
Our duty perfectly.

Scrub out, chaps, and ask them
To take her to recovery;
Let's hope she wakes to see
Another hopeless day.

[04.08.16]

Between Worlds

I met him at midnight
In a mist-shrouded wood.
He beckoned me to dance
To a lilting étude.

We swayed to the music
In a haunting embrace.
I felt that I knew him,
Though had not seen his face.

He opened his black cloak
And I entered a land
Where pain was converted
Into contraband.

I went to the goblins
Who held all the potions
And charmingly pledged
My deepest devotion.

I drank and observed
As my body unfurled.
Now armed with the power,
I move between worlds.

[20.08.16]

Ghostly Presence In The Hall

It is my mansion on the hill;
Magnificent and solitary.
I gaze from the upper window
At the garden and distant sea.

I hear the sound of the rocking horse,
Creaking gently as the children play;
Their voices carrying like music
On a sultry summer day.

And the sweet smell of roses
Fills the air and carries me
To another time, another place
In the forefront of my memory.

He was dressed in uniform
When he left on that winter's day.
I held him for the longest time
Then watched him as he walked away.

I waited for a century
For my lover to return;
The clock ticking endlessly
But he never did come home.

I can hear the children running,
Responding to their mother's call.
They cannot see me but they sense
The ghostly presence in the hall.

[21.08.16]

Spark of Light

I'll stay with you forever,
If you'll take me to that strange place
Where I danced for you in silk and lace.

We thought we'd brought the heavens down
With that euphoric rush of bliss,
With that soul-satisfying kiss.

Still I love you and I ride
In chariots to the star-filled sky;
That spark of light can never die.

[26.08.16]

Life Confined

The swish of movement in a strange place,
I feel the contours of your face,
The scent of flowers as petals fall
On the carcass rotting in the hall.

They are charging home as the restless sea
Responds in rapturous symphony;
A surge of dreamers duly glean
A swathe of images best unseen.

The restless night, all safety gone
To wither in its fetid tomb.
One swift adventure more refined
Than a century with life confined.

[21.09.16]

Lost Heritage

Sodden peat bogs and driving rain,
The smell of slurry in the wind,
A great expanse of vibrant green
And my heritage left unseen.

So I am drifting evermore
A long, long way from Ireland's shore;
Pandering to the part of me
That yearns for a sense of family.

[22.09.16]

An Unfamiliar Beat

I cannot feel the earth beneath my feet
As we dance to an unfamiliar beat.
Snowflakes are sparkling and swirling above
The palpable mass of innocent love:

To wisdom it inextricably binds
And captures the most ingenious minds,
Which labour in selfless alacrity
For the advancement of humanity;

And the humble poet tries to glean
The beauty from each chaotic scene,
Alluding to truths that flutter and bend,
Like shadows in the gathering wind.

[01.10.16]

Bereft

I am bereft
Without your magic,
Without the hurricane
Of your presence.

For twenty-two years
Your voice has cut through
London's screaming noise,
And the black of all blackness
Suffocates.

I want to rip out these innards
And crush these brittle bones;
Then run to you,
Either to fly free
Or be oblivious
To the supreme peace.

[13.11.16]

Resignation

I wake and sleep in solitude,
Entrenched in melancholy's mire.
It was folly to expect that
Further horrors would not transpire.

The days are a mighty python
That crushes till I gasp for breath,
The night a sinister phantom
That taunts with the promise of death.

And though I have stood on a mountain
And railed at my torment and pain,
I descended with resignation
To the world and its chaos again.

[30.12.16]

The Glittering Sword

A cloak of serpents writhing zealously
On the contours of her ample body.
The devil's comrades dancing in chains,
Enthralled by melodramatic strains.

Tapestries hang in rooms underground,
Where nefarious voices resound.
The darkness emits a merciless claw
That tears at the humanistic flaw.

The creatures awake, devoid of intent,
Surrendered to disillusionment.
The glittering sword is raised from the sand
And placed in the waiting warrior's hand.

[07.01.17]

Loyalty

It is the potency of torture
That evokes me to move my pen.
I plead with faithless happiness
To awaken in me again.

No gifts of honour and kindness
Have gracefully drifted my way.
No dreams have come to fruition
In the course of the longest day.

At least the music is soothing
And sleep will soon come for me.
When I wake you will be waiting
With unfaltering loyalty.

[11.01.17, To Bashkim]

Brink of An Unknown Dawn

My eerie dalliances with you
Are now becoming commonplace;
Existence thwarted as you lay
Your cold, dead hand upon my face.

In acquiescence, I reside
In ruinous, solitary days;
Courting tedium as though it held
The brightest of the sun's bright rays:

Criticising and applauding
As I watch the world go by,
Repetitious in a chaos
That only Nature can defy.

And each antithesis reminds me
Of a fickle predisposition
To plump for the transient pleasure
That deflects from life's true vision.

Be that as it may, let us return
To our strange and perilous bond;
You hold the reins and mercilessly
Draw me to the brink of an unknown dawn.

[05.02.17]

Radiance

Despite the barbarism and insanity
That have seeped into the consciousness of humankind,
Love continues to prevail over hate.
Despite the ravages of modern life
On Planet Earth and its inhabitants,
Nature continues to proliferate.

All solutions and hopes of happiness
Lie in the act of cooperation,
And salvation can never come too late.
The bridge of life is short but blessed
With radiance that blinds the naked eye
And wonders to silently contemplate.

[22.02.17]

Fragile Landscape

She's floating on an ocean
Of blood-stained red,
Sound of the sullen muse
Silenced in that watery bed;

The shrill loneliness of
A thousand planes and cars
Muted as she faces
Upwards to the stars.

Too many sounds driven
Into the mind's fragile landscape,
And seemingly only
One way to escape.

She would have loved
The birds' sweet symphony
That soothed the heart
Of the sleepless city.

[26.02.17]

Attainment of Truth

Not a Freudian slip;
Simply in the grip
Of unabridged honesty.
Perception edgy;
Therefore, I can see
Into another reality.

Summer lost in a haze
Of mania and desperation,
Sitting like a lonely vagabond
In the deserted railway station.

Cogs turning, the great
Machine whirring;
The frail ones swallowed up
By the men in suits,
In the pursuit of power;
Monstrous avarice
In every waking hour.

Slide beneath the sheets before
The midnight onset
Of dissonance.
Falling into deep, internal space
Is paramount to
The attainment of Truth.

[08.03.17]

Imaginings

It must have been but a dream:
The taste of sea salt and freedom,
The glow of the morning sun;
A bitter-sweet encounter
When hope frequents a humble home.

I might only have imagined
That you stepped out of a rainbow
When the world's eyes were turned away.
The breeze gifted to me the sound
Of your lyrical soliloquy.

It might just have been a mirage,
Evoked by the strain of living
And the nuance of a time and place;
It might have been one final,
Unavailing attempt at solace.

[26.04.17]

Revival

Sometimes only music is needed;
No words to confound the melody
Or melancholy;
No brow-beating to obstruct
The unveiling of the beauty:

No conductor to carry the
Streams of consciousness
Into the great universal ocean;
No grand swathes of motion
To transport the lifeless vessel.

The flow will rise and cascade
All by itself, unaided;
And the smallest droplets
Will charge even the weariest
Into the sweetest revival.

[27.05.17]

Pearls

Translucent pearls placed in my hand
By an empress with flaxen hair;
The swish of her silken dress hypnotic
As it trails in the foaming sea.

The beach deserted and the stars
Relishing their supremacy,
Invoking the solitary wanderer's desire
To run with the raging rivers
And merge with the endless sky.

THEN:

Tick-tock, back to earth
And the stroll through the quiet street,
And the sound of a pearl dropping at his feet.

[10.06.17]

Unfettered

Not one of the herd,
Not to be tamed
Or penned,
Or pastured on a land
That is constrained.

More like the bird
With scant companionship
But free to soar
In limitless expanses.

But most of all
Akin to the fortress
With all doors flung open
And the great storm of life
Flowing unfettered.

[20.06.17]

Secrets

It seems that I should be my self-confessor,
For who can withstand these diabolical topics?
Mirrors of mortality that they are.

I cannot maintain the momentum;
Even the breath of life eludes me,
And the futility of petition screeches
In the vacant internal space,
Wherein the only option is exploration,
Till the glistening treasures appear -

Then I can tell you the secrets
In the midst of the deep, indigo night,
When love has pervaded all kingdoms.

[29.06.17]

Philosophical Feast

No applause for consciousness
And its gross limitations;
Got to stretch it, be expansive,
Embrace the implications.

The secret lies in reverie
When all activity has ceased -
No preparation is required
For this philosophical feast.

We'll all be waiting and atuned
To that specific frequency.
Mere words and thoughts will melt in light
Of their complete redundancy.

[05.07.17]

Abandon

I can hear Druidic chanting
And the drums beating far away.
I can see beyond the mountains
To the dawn of a better day.

I feel the ocean rushing through me
In one almighty cleansing wave.
I hold the reins of chariots
That serve as vessels for the brave.

I maximise the world of dreams
To visit those I can't attend.
What can my body be but broken
When my soul's abandon knows no end?

[05.07.17]

Up From The Skies

In 1983 A Merman I Should Turn To Be,
For I'm a Voodoo Chile from a new reality.
I found my Freedom Up From the Skies
When the Fire lit up in her Gypsy Eyes.

And The Gods Made Love on a Little Wing
Where the Third Stone From The Sun was
Drifting;
They were as Bold As Love and Stone Free,
Like a Foxey Lady with EXP.

Have You Ever Been To Electric Ladyland?
Are You Experienced enough to understand
How the Moon Turns The Tides, Gently, Gently
Away
And The Wind Cries Mary on a magical day?

If Six Was Nine when the world was appraised
In a Roomful of Mirrors in a Purple Haze,
You could fly to infinity with Slight Return
And float in the Land of the New Rising Sun.

[19.07.17 – 21.07.17]
Song titles by Jimi Hendrix

Bright Rays of Truth

Mystical Aurora, flashing green,
Dancing spirits on a sky-screen;
Beyond the limits of fragile Earth,
Borne of the sun's omnipotent breadth.

Red star burning for eternity,
Till I am you and you are me;
Merged with the deep, and companionless;
No life or death as our honoured guest.

And the shipwreck lies with faded blooms
In the world below, in the lonely rooms
Where wraiths and poets engage in vain thoughts
Of bright rays of Truth that cannot be sought.

[23.07.17]

False Hope

The pain, discomfort,
Malaise of the bowel.
Throw in the towel -
Hurl the afflicted body
Off that stunning Menai Bridge,

Or cling to the accursed hope,
Like the tight-rope walker
Dangerously close to falling off
That flimsy perch.

Lying in the ditch again,
In the gutter at just fifteen.
Now fifty-two and finally
Loosening my grip on that false hope;
The scourge of many a blighted life.

[24.07.17]

The Glittering Orb

This tiredness is killing me;
Perhaps even literally.
Summer is unpredictable
And she is still delectable
As she dances to Brown-Eyed Girl.

I see beyond the fog and rain,
Beyond the decades and the pain;
Two vibrant siblings in the throes
                              of dreams
And wild imaginings.

She is in the world alone now,
Reminiscing about the town
That ultimately brought them down.
He is in a forest in the air,
In the darkest night, and everywhere:

He holds the moon in his outstretched palm;
The glittering orb that guides her home.

[28.07.17]

Afflicted

I love you in the daytime,
When the wind howls through
My treasured home in Ynys Môn.
I love you as I gaze upon
      the turbulent sea;
Your lovely face freeze-framed
In the midst of that mercurial reverie.

I love you in the black of night,
When the world is asleep
And my aching bones, not old
But weary beyond their years,
Impress upon me the ephemeral
      nature of all things.

I am taken back to the beginning:
The small, naked boy in the kitchen sink,
Shivering and baffled by the weekly ritual.
My heart simultaneously bursts
      with joy and pain,
And in that moment I am not so
      afflicted by your death.

[02.08.17, To John]

Who I Am

Clippity-clop, the world has stopped,
For logical reason or fate,
I dream of that Gothic seascape
Hanging over the fireplace,
And my own virtuoso performance
                on the piano;
Seated in my red velvet gown,
With the sound of miracles encroaching
                upon the gloom.

Come now to my silent rooms
And speak to me in hushed Celtic tones
That signify a rare form of significance.
Let me unravel in the Cymrian rain
And finally remember who I am.

[05.08.17]

Unearthly Dancer

I couldn't watch you fade away,
Didn't have that supreme courage;
Consequently lost eight thousand days
And sank into the unreachable.

How glorious now to wander
In these rooms of my one true home!
The sight of Heaven in the distance,
And your unmistakeable presence.

Your enigmatic voice telling me
That everything is as it should be;
All expansive moments moving
In perfect synchronicity.

And though they shall reprimand me
For my poetic abstraction,
The muse provides a stalwart guide;
Unearthly dancer at my side.

[09.08.17]

Onslaught

There's a hole in my garden
That I just can't seem to fill;
I cover it with earth but
               in the morning
There it is, gaping like
               an exposed wound.

I sense that the birds claw out
               its contents;
Throwing up the dirt and dead leaves
And dragging them into the sunshine,
But some whirling vortex below
Keeps sucking them back
               into the darkness.

It seems to be an aberration of nature;
The smallest of black holes
On a planet that doesn't exist.

A few shards of daylight
Filter through the black-out curtains.
I awake with the feeling of having
               frequented some unknown land.
The first cup of tea tastes so good
As I await the onslaught of pain.

[15.08.17]

Eternal Space

My mind wanders away:
When I'm staring at the small trees
                waving in the wind;
When the flowering shrubs are in
                      full bloom
And the butterflies are fluttering overhead.

My emotions start to stray:
When I find one of your
              long-lost letters
In the final box unpacked
              from the garage
On a blustery, sunny day.

I try not to wither
When your image floods
       every corner of my mind.
I try to find the meaning
       in the mundane moments
That are sometimes moored
             in eternal space.

[18.08.17]

Stilled

I forgot to flatten my palm
And that old nag tried to swallow my hand
Along with the rotting apple.

Back at the house, the maternal one
At the kitchen sink, engaged in some domestic
activity. Heavy odour in the air,
Scent of incest from a bygone era.

Drunk on cider in the evening;
Muscled cousin boasting of martial arts
And tying his black belt around my small waist;
Another familial flirtation.

Out-of-body sensation;
Waiting for the letter to drop through the door
For the corpse laid on the floor;
Breath and poisonous thoughts now stilled.

Cars and people pass the tortured bride,
Scanning eyes for signs of gallantry.
Don't ask the Nomad about her past exploits.

Lost kingdom, rat-infested daydreams,
Peace comes at a premium.
The urban cockerel disrupts the invalid's sleep.

The midnight coach doesn't travel
To those far-flung destinations.
I think you've killed him.

[18.08.17]

Misguided

Part I

Every day I pay the cost
To you, an oblivious host.
I have escaped insanity
Because it is afraid of me.

The followers are muted and mild,
Swallowing the propaganda
Like wild gaggles of geese
Who function automatically;
Incapable of introspection
Or critique of the powers-that-be.

Maybe all hope rests with the young
Who have not sacrificed their moral code
For the proverbial pot of gold
Or, more dangerously, fallen prey
To some political popinjay.

Part II

I saw a GP today -
She was clearly terrified
By my medical history.
Wanted to send me back to London
For oncology follow-up:
Talk about pass-the-buck -
A monumental head-fuck!

[23.08.17]

Nobody's Hero

He won't be anyone's hero
Till you pluck him from
                that blackened slum.
No point in waiting quarter of a century
And presenting him with the
                suited psychiatrist
Who is still dreaming of Oxford's spires:

Too many scars by then,
Too many dopamine rushes
                in unsafe places.
The Gods don't make love
                on his patch -
It is too densely populated
By the dark-eyed ones
            with the brown sugar.

If that's not your bag,
Drown in the hard liquor
Till your skull smashes
                on the pavement
And the gushing blood
           is of no consequence.

There but for the grace of [   ];
He seems to have his favourites.

[28.08.17]

Heady Scent of Freedom

A speck in space, member of the human race;
Lone figure on the beach before the storm.
Complex whirrings of the brain -
A mystery to everyone.

The prefrontal cortex hailed as
The holy grail of consciousness;
The seat of knowledge and invention,
Innovation and progression -
Until the cracks began to show:

The ego soared and the attainment of power
Became the ultimate goal;
Injustice the order of the day -
The elite thriving in their bright mansions
While the masses struggle to survive.

Fame and celebrity have insidiously
Crept into the minds of the young,
For whom the art of communication
Is irrevocably entwined with technology;
Face-to-face and the human touch
Becoming an anomaly.

The observer, who has stepped off the treadmill,
Gazes upon the great expanse of Irish Sea
And breathes in the heady scent of freedom.

[08.09.17]

Purple

The colour purple:
Mysterious, soothing;
Distracts from all else.

Jimi Hendrix, Purple Haze,
The seventeen-year old in
      hippy gear,
The beautiful one with the
      straw-coloured hair,
The vastness of the sky.

Only later, other things
      come into view:
The rolling hills, fir trees,
Bright-coloured meadow.
But the fence has a hue
      of purple.

Back to the soothing colour
Of youth and vibrancy,
The beauty of the sibling relationship,
Hopes for the future.

The mind becomes expansive,
Obliterating time and space;
A split-second of infinity
Then the sun comes into view.

Chase out the shadows
Before the hour of midnight descends.

[09.09.17]

The Great Melting Pot

Presented with the South Stack,
I am taken back quarter of a century,
Travelling in a whirlwind
Back to the cliffs of Land's End.

Down the steep steps, the late summer breeze
Guides me toward the distant lighthouse,
With Joy at my side - her strong presence
Like life-affirming medicine.

Gazing upon such splendour,
The ego is obliterated
By that sense of oneness;
That great melting pot
Into which we all must descend.

[12.09.17]

Stirrings of Life

A single snowdrop
Fell into the sea
Unnoticed.
Beneath the surface
A dangerous fracas;
Light shifting to dark.

In the mute stillness
The nightmares surface,
Awake too soon.

Turn on the light,
Wait for the dawn
And stirrings of life.

[12.09.17]

Unconditionally

I was as blue as I could be
But I loved him unconditionally.
I forgot the world and lost myself
In the universe of his eyes,
And there began my gradual demise.

I waited for a symphony
That could raise the heart
To the glories of infinity,
But all I heard were shallow calls
In the musty ruins of hallowed halls.

And the love, once sacred, was polarised
Till the bond was broken
By the mighty sword
That masquerades as reality;
Still I loved him unconditionally.

[23.09.17]

I Think of You

I think of you when the daylight
Is dimming into evening
And I'm weary from the long day.
I think of you when I close my eyes
And listen to the symphony.

It is impossible to say why
You should endure such suffering
When others thrive in happiness.
It is impossible to fathom
Life's vulgar inequalities.

They labelled it cerebral palsy,
Said you'd only make it to twenty one,
But your soul was of a greater might
Than nature or even life itself;
Bathed in its eternal light.

You could not hold us together,
A family that simply fell apart.
I only wish there had been some pleasure
To attenuate the turmoil
Of that most artless art.

I wish you had had the chances,
Like others, to pursue your dreams,
And to have felt love's rapturous glow.
I wish the world had met you and witnessed
What only we, your siblings, know.

You are a hero of unending grace,
Who was forced to court adversity.
You will rest in a celestial place;
And I beg you, dearest brother,
To live on in spirit, to dwell with me.

[14.10.17, To Mickey]

Final Moondance

You speak to me as though
I were a separate person;
I am you, wandering around these rooms.

You, as a separate entity,
Are in the wild winds
And the rustle of the trees,
You are in the bright sunshine
And the silver shimmer of the sea.

We are all bound by souls
That recognise each other at first sight,
And the balm of friendship
Soothes the horrors of a previous life.

Let's have one final moondance
Before the fire fades to an ember.

[16.10.17]

Tantalising Glimpse

Retreat – inwards, backwards,
Childhood thwarted by war
                or other atrocities.
Shatter the usual structure,
Leave conventionality behind.

Imagination and Innocence,
All the universes in the bright blue
                of Irish eyes,

A tantalising glimpse...

[16.10.17]

View of My Deeper Aspect

Please stay within the view of my deeper aspect,
Otherwise I will fall into the dark chasm
That annihilates the will to carry on.

I was once given to a romanticism
That led to perilous peaks and troughs.
I was wise not to have divulged this
                to the medics
Who look for clues in their ridiculous
                diagnostic manuals.

The privileged ones have no real
                concept of suffering
Or the way in which people lie shattered
                and broken
From the harsh realities of life.

"Every day above ground is a good day,"
Said the corrupt cop in 'Scarface'.
I repeat this mantra when I am on
                the verge of giving up.

Please stay within the view of my deeper aspect.

[22.10.17]

Melancholic Sense of Forever

It's all so pretty in Anglesey,
But let me live;
Let me run toward the sea
And kiss the mountains
With a single leap.

Let the stars whisper to me
Of angels who ride
On the far side of the moon.
Give me another surge of energy
Before I melt into the dust.

I am locked in your heart,
Present in all your rooms.
We are everywhere, as one;
Wrapped in a sweet
Melancholic sense of forever.

[31.10.17]

Pathological Bourgeoisie

Revel in your black tie events -
The Dom Perignon and canapés.
Speak of the lower classes
With that patronising smile on your face:

"They do it to themselves, you know -
Fuck up their lives, then drain the system.
What of the hunger and squalor?
Not our duty to assist them.

Now, back to important matters at hand -
Did you check the Dow-Jones today?
Did you uphold the strict code of honour
Of the pathological bourgeoisie?"

[01.11.17]

Dimensional Shift

I awake to daylight
But can't get out of bed.
The universe crushes me
Till I am nothing but a speck.

It would just take a splurge
               of courage
To effect a dimensional shift.
We would stroll and kick
               autumn leaves
And have no knowledge
Of all that had gone before.

[13.11.17]

Earthy Aroma of Youth

It is a rare event these days –
encountering the scent of patchouli.
It was even considered hippyish
when I was wearing the oil
in that summer of 1982.
I used to buy the dark little bottle
of Spiritual Sky from the exotic shop
not far from our flat in Glasgow's West End.

Do you remember it?:
the large, spartan room with the high ceilings
and poster of Jimi Hendrix by the window;
your tiny annexe that could only hold
the single bed and rickety chest of drawers;
our flatmates, the African students,
with their bright, flamboyant clothing;
and the strange combined odours
of curried chicken and cannabis.

Do you remember our long strolls
through Kelvingrove Park?;
a chance to breathe in the heady scents of nature
and speak of our dreams for a better future.

You only made it to twenty-six,
your beauty taken from this world by your own hand.
Now, the memories keep me afloat
when I am drowning, and the deep,
earthy aroma of our youth brings me back to life.

[17.11.17, To John]

Take Me Home

When I miss you the world is grey;
There are no hues or scents,
Nothing makes a difference.

I want to scream into the gaping silence.
I want to stretch my hand through the ether
And pull you back onto this earthly plane.

The world is buckling
Under the strain of your absence,
Withering without your love.

The clock ticks its meaningless repetition
And I repeat my meaningless existence
As I wait for you to take me home.

[17.11.17]

Already Dead

"You move between idealism
And nihilism," he said.
"You're manic-depressive,"
Another one posited.

In these statements there is little scope
For further interpretation
Or concept of external means
Of character annihilation.

Maybe the world sucked me in
And spat me out so many times
That I couldn't see the road ahead.
Now it's all so hauntingly still -
Maybe I'm already dead.

[20.11.17]

Lost Faith In Humanity

I have lost all faith in humanity:
The implication is that I chose
To exist as that lamb to the slaughter;
That I placed myself in the devil's hands,
Knelt at that diabolical altar.

The implication is that my brother
Chose to internalise the violence
That set a wreckage to his foundation;
That deprived him of stability
Or the merest hint of expectation.

There was no saviour for him as there was for me,
No blossom in the concrete wilderness
Or promise of love in the stifled breath.
When the darkness reigned and all hope was gone,
He could not resist the pull of death.

I have lost all faith in humanity:
For the systematic failures
And the world that permitted him to die.
He took my essence to his early grave,
He took the life from my deadened eyes.

[27.11.17, To John]

What Can I Do?

The moon, obscured by wintry-white clouds
On this frosty day in December.
What can I do but wistfully smile?
What can I do but remember?

The garden is withering
But cannot be revived by me.
It is surprising that nature
Has given me half a century.

Detached, separated, isolated;
Can't go back but nothing ahead.
The wailing of his 'Bleeding Heart'
Abates the screaming in my head.

[04.12.17]

Gateway To Liberty

There was never any Truth or Meaning;
It was all just a constructed vision -
The human desire to pursue a dream
In the hollowness of a vacuum:

Where the moon and stars and the universe
Implode with the sound of a dying breath;
Where the comfort of a soothing word
Is finally of no consequence.

That dreaded chasm of a former day
Is the perfect bedfellow for decay:
A passage in the dark that proves to be
The only gateway to liberty.

[04.12.17]

Breathless

Survival guilt – the parasite
That is never truly sated.
Catastrophic consequence;
Eyes dulled, lifeless,
The body hanging by a thread.

Even the mighty
Are brought to their knees,
Even the shadows retreat in terror.

Bones withered, worn by time,
Existence played out
In a strange, apocalyptic paradigm.

Reprieve in the multi-coloured skyline
That illuminates the vast, rolling sea;
Breathless with anticipation
Of all that lies beyond the self.

[26.12.17]

Dark Angel

You are my dark angel,
Crouched beneath a crescent moon;
Oceanic brilliance
In captivating eyes.

You hold aloft a sabre
That symbolises freedom;
The supernatural goal
Of the wild Celtic soul.

Days of churning, mourning,
Swept up in the howling wind.
Sleep and all other pleasures
The briefest of flirtations.

You are my dark angel,
Seated at my silent bed;
A temptress beguiling
But just beyond my reach.

[31.12.17]

The Life

He said "the moonbeams kiss the sea"*
And I believed it to be true;
Wandering under a romantic cloud
While the world almost beat me to death.

I'm wasted now – no more lipstick
Or glamorous attire,
No lover to enthrall me with charm
And wild sweeping gestures.

Even his magnificent strains
Of Voodoo Chile (Slight Return)
Can only raise a wry smile
For the life that once ran through
                our youthful veins.

[31.12.17]

*From 'Love's Philosophy' (Percy Bysshe Shelley, 1819).

Today's Bulletin

Black
Emptiness
Low
Lower than low
Shrinking
Speck
Invisible
Still feeling
Pain

[31.12.17]

Anglesey Eyes

Your eyes, as blue as the mystical sea,
Enrapture and devour my soul.
One glimpse of you in the morning light
And the anchor of the mundane
Drifts like flotsam on a smooth summer tide.

The scent of honeysuckle is conjured
By a mind that slept for a decade or more;
The urge to dance on a crowded dance-floor,
To feel your strength and energy
Reverberate in the core of me.

Your face emerges in my swirling dreams;
Harbingers of fortitude and the magic of
                              optimism.
The chill of winter gives rise to the new life in
                              Spring
And your blue eyes are eternally etched in
                              everything.

[25.01.18]

The Portal of Sleep

It is a new beginning
In which the dawn passes me by
And I sway in the luxury of timelessness:
Swathes of harmony,
Red skies adorned
With the hallowed presence of the moon.

Your spirit-self takes me
To the heart of the dark wood,
Where the ghosts of past lovers
Weave between paths of ethereal lands.
I hear their whisperings
As midnight beckons to the portal of sleep.

[27.01.18]

Passing Through

Welsh mountains, firmly in my view;
Fresh, snow-capped, permanent.
I'm passing through;
A temporary marker in your life,
And gladly fading;
The soil, neatly parted and waiting,
Like a lifeless womb.

Just one last surge of memories:
A heyday – a glorious dream,
Then the finale,
          BLACK.

[19.02.18]

Debris

He saw miracles every day.
Either I can't see any,
Or I can't see their purpose.

Humankind has lost
It's sense of humanity;
Hurtling at great speed towards
The edge of destruction.

The gatekeepers of Hell
Are spitting venom
At the sick and downtrodden,
And the clergy anoint
With tainted intent.

It's either battle or retreat,
Inflict or empathise,
Falter under the weight of cynicism
Or reconvene;
Find a new doctrine
Before the mighty hand of time
Has swept away all its debris.

[26.03.18]

Uncharted Territory

No firm basis,
Skirting around the edges,
Rooted but free-falling:
Everyone's Celtic darling
Coming apart at the seams,
A hurricane in a small package.

No filter, slightly off kilter.
Don't play with metaphor
When the Muse's wrecking ball
Is breaking down all barriers;
Thanatos rushing to the fore,
Pushing at the door of insanity.

Moments of anchorage
In eyes that carry legends
And seize upon the eternal
That runs through veins of fire.

Pull her roots down firmly
Into your Welsh ground.
There is a fledgling waiting to sore
In uncharted territory.

[06.04.18]

The Magic of Ynys Môn

I'm home at last,
In the place where dreams ride
On the wanton sea,
And elegant ladies gaze
Through stained-glass windows
At their flowering shrubbery.

The piece from Rigoletto
Playing on the piano
In the sunlit room
Flows from my own hands,
As I hear the distant voice
Of the rugged Welsh man.

And how still the night!
When my soul laments
But still spurs me on;
Attuned to the magic
Of Ynys Môn.

[24.05.18]

Inconsequential Living

You need to come home to me;
To bring that sweet sense
Of the earth shifting.
I need to see those eyes
That shame the stars
And convey their yearnings
Without a single word.

I want to be your lover
Before the treacherous breath of time
Withers me as it withers all.
One moment in that tornado-like rush
And I will forego a decade
Of inconsequential living.

[28.05.18]

Printed in Great Britain
by Amazon